Wishing you moments
of quiet joy
My Best,
Anne

The Monk and the Goddess

僧與神

The Monk and the Goddess

M. Anne Knoll

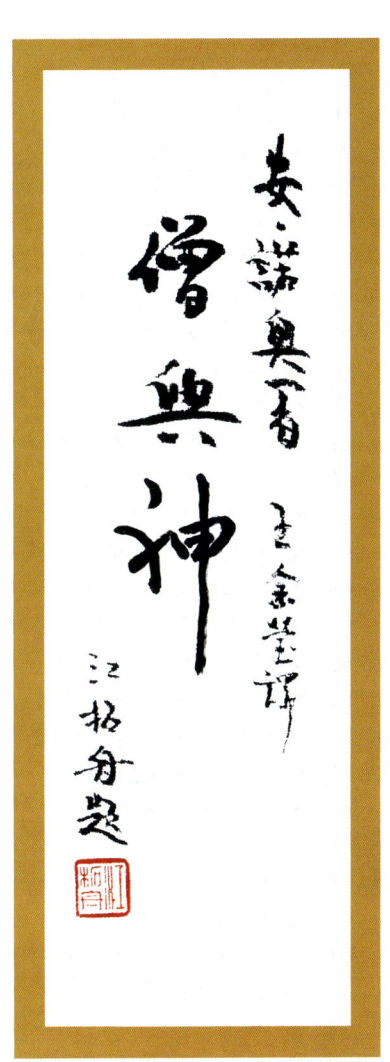

Huaguang Art and Cultural Center

© 2003 M. Anne Knoll

All rights reserved. According to USA and international copyright laws, no part of this publication may be reproduced or transmitted in any form or by any means, electronic or mechanical, including photocopy, recording, or any information storage and retrieval system, without permission in writing from the author.

First Edition

Photography and Story: M. Anne Knoll
Translation: Dr. Jin Ying Wang
Calligraphy and Artwork: Zhe-zhou Jiang

ISBN# 0-9755266-1-8

Printed in China

"I was astonished by the spirit of the monk, and torn by the soul of the goddess."
Zhe-zhou Jiang

Foreword
Bi-Fang
(Zhe-zhou Jiang)

On January 18, 2003 the twelve cherished students of "The Scholars of the Spring" Fine Art Genre, gathered at an artist reception to celebrate my birthday. It was at that party when I first met Anne Knoll, the distinguished director of the Ritz Art Gallery. She was refined and intelligent. We were not able to engage in a suitable conversation that day, because I was preoccupied with many activities.

The Gallery is housed in a theatre; so, after the celebration, everyone went in to see the play <u>Annie Get Your Gun</u>. Prior to the opening of the show, I was amazed when the members of the audience, more than four hundred people, exclaimed "Happy Birthday" to me. For a moment, my mind returned to China and I felt like the monk in Anne's book, one having been on a long journey-a journey that had brought him through the loss of his father at age three, and finally the death of his mother. My thoughts were interrupted when my young son Louis stood up and made shooting sounds, like some of the characters in the play, which made everyone laugh. But what was also interesting and fortuitous was the fact that the strong heroine of this play was also named Anne.

After half a year, I received a phone call from Anne asking if I would do the calligraphy for the title of her creation The Monk and the Goddess, which was a story accompanied by strong photographs. We met to discuss it. I did not consider my handwriting to be intact, but I couldn't refuse her sincere request. Now that I am familiar with her work, I recall the lingering scene of our meeting, when "astonished by the spirit of the monk, and torn by the soul of the goddess" happened that day.

At the beginning, I wrote only three words in Chinese calligraphy for the title. Later, I was deeply moved while reading the touchable story and seeing the beautiful photographs in Anne's book. The translation, too, was elegant. It had been done by Jin Ying Wang M.D., Ph.D. whose father is a well-known writer and calligrapher in China. After reading both, I seized the impulse to incorporate both their names in calligraphy as part of the cover design for the book.

Anne also asked if I would create a special design, which would be used on the pages in the book where no photograph appeared. Even though I call myself an art designer, this was not easy for me. In the past, I had made several commissioned designs like the Association for Asian and African Writers design, The "Golden Fish Bowl" design for the Franklin Mint, an enamel Dragon Dish, and a word design for the well-known writer Anchee Min. All of the designs had been completed in twenty-four hours as requested by my supervisors.

This time, however, I spent several weeks thinking and sketching. The story and photographs moved me very much. Thirty sketches came out and finally a new design was created. I present this new design to my art and calligraphy ancestors, Cang Jie who created Chinese letters that resembled pictures 5000 years ago, and to Lisi of the Qiang Dynasty who created Chinese calligraphy as we know it today. I also offer my work for my friends and future generations. I will live up to the great expectation and kindness of Anne Knoll.

1 admire Anne Knoll. She has created perfect harmony, graced with "deep thinking," using both art and words. I praise the exquisite and meaningful translation into Chinese by Dr. Jin Ying Wang. This publication is not only photographs and a story with poetic words but it is a real aphorism that is both classic and contemporary. Their contribution for the propagation and blending of Western and Eastern cultures, and the development of world peace is absolutely great! May people be inspired for generations to come!

驚僧魄　泣神魂
——安－諾奧攝影詩集《僧與神》序

碧舫

今年一月十八日，《春天的使者》畫派的艾汶、諾瑪、朵瑞茜、杰歐、帕蒂、艾琳、敏克、艾倫、比垂斯等十二位得意門生，在瑞斯畫廊爲我慶生。會上我初見安－諾奧女士，她是那裏的畫廊主任，語不在多，顯得謙恭有禮，甚有内功。她看我忙，沒有多説什麼。

會後，在旁邊劇場觀看紐約四十二街保留劇目《安接過你的槍》，當四百余人歡呼着祝我生日快樂，令我這三歲喪父，近年喪母的"遠行僧"驚异不已！艫兒又站在座位上模仿槍擊聲，使場内高潮迭起。巧得很，主角的名字也叫安。

半年之後，我接到了安的電話，問我是否願意爲她的作品《僧與神》用書法題名。我自知字丑，却奈不過她誠心摯意地再三請懇。使我想起了那日驚僧魄，而又泣神魂的難忘場面，只好"諸葛亮披戰袍"倉惶應下了。

在書的封面設計上，先題了書名的三個字，可是越看安的詩情畫意越忍不住添寫了她的大名。後來看了中國名作家和書法家之女，醫學博士王金瑩的優美譯詩，又感動地題上了她的芳名。安又讓我在詩圖空白處設計個圖案，却難煞了多年來自稱藝術設計師的我。當年《長城香烟》，《北京醬醋系列》，《亞非記協會徽》等，直到林達－瑞斯尼克讓我設計的《金魚缸系列》和《景泰藍龍盤》及爲名作家閔安琪設計的《門内海外好文章》篆文，都是在老板們的授意下，二十四小時内完成的。這次構思，花費了數周之久，構畫了三十草圖，總算在僧敲神助之下，完成了一個新字的創造，呈現給倉頡、李斯先師及天下友人和"敵人"點評笑納，也算没有辜負安－諾奧的重托和美意。

我贊賞安－諾奧巧妙地在藝術和文字上都求取了優美地和諧和深刻地沉思；我贊嘆王金瑩博士譯文的精致和隽永筆調。這不僅是一部散文詩，更象是鏤古鑄今的格言！她們對東西方文化的傳播和交融，以及對世界和平的發展功不可没。

二零零三年九月十日先父五十四周年忌辰凌晨二時

Acknowledgements

My gift to each of the following is gratitude. My challenge is expressing it.

My Family — *for their presence in my life.*

Jeff Roberts and Joanne Mullin-McBride — *for their open-hearted compassion and willingness to give themselves over completely to the Monk and the Goddess, transcending the limits of speech and working only within the realm of touch. Amazing, both.*

Zhe-zhou Jiang/Huaguang Art and Cultural Center — *for his beautiful calligraphy and artwork, his generosity of spirit, his infectious enthusiasm, and for providing the possibility of a bi-lingual book publication.*

Dr. Jin Ying Wang — *for her thoughtful attention to my words in translation.*

Yin-Feng Zhang — *for her contribution to my book printing.*

Gary Collings — *for his patient mentorship.*

The Members of The Artist Conference Network — *for their on-going coaching, encouragement, and love.*

Stan James and Emil Sheth/Cresent Photo Lab — *for their attention to detail.*

Zen Mountain Monastery and Fire Lotus Temple — *for their existence.*

The Fabulous Five – *for their unconditional love and support.*

我感激地把禮物獻給大家，很難以表達我的謝意。

　　我的家人——因爲他們存在于我的生命中。
　　杰夫－羅伯特和喬尼亞－慕林麥克布萊德——對于他們全心全意地同情和情願獻出自身給"僧與神"，和超越語言交流限制僅用身體接觸完成拍攝工作。兩人的表現都是令人驚奇的。
　　江柘舟／華光文化藝術中心——對于他唯美的書法和藝術設計，他慷慨的精神和積極熱心，以及使本書能以兩種語言文字出版。
　　王金瑩博士——對于她所作出的字斟句酌地文字翻譯。
　　張寅峰——對于本書的出版和發行做了大量的工作。
　　該瑞－考林斯——對于他耐心的顧問指導作用。
　　藝術家商議網的成員們——對于他們持續地指導，鼓勵和愛護。
　　斯坦－詹姆斯和愛密歐－西斯／克瑞森特照片實驗室——對于他們的仔細認真。
　　譜山修道院和火蓮寺——對于他們的存在。
　　神奇五人團——對于他們無條件地愛護和支持。

M. Anne Knoll

The Monk and the Goddess has been, from the beginning, a project without intention. It led me; I did not lead it. In retrospect, the process seemed the reverse of what we might think of as the natural order of things. The photo shoot came first; the story followed.

Responding to the idea that there was a monk with three doubts and a goddess who would transform herself into a human with three longings, I brought together two friends of mine who had never met. The guidelines for the shoot were that they could not speak to one another for the duration of the photo session, nor see one another's faces except in rare moments, since they would be positioned one in front of the other. They could rely only on the connection of touch. It was up to them to be present and respond.

We talked a bit. They dressed. It began. Six hours later, it was complete. We were speechless. We were changed. For each of the three of us, it was a transformational experience of trust, compassion, love and the healing power of kindness. I didn't know what my images would reveal, but I knew what I had witnessed through my lens.

The results? Quiet amazement, as we sat witness to what was offered in the images. Each portrait whispered, sang, shouted, even danced bits of a story I had yet to write. In the following months, I remained open to flickers of images, like Tinkerbells dancing across water. I gathered them up. I assembled the details — and a journey of enlightment emerged. A journey as much for myself as for the Monk and the Goddess.

The process has offered me a gift, which I share with you within these pages.

安－諾奧

　　《僧與神》這部作品在創作之初，是一個没有引起關注的題目，它引導我而我没有引導它。回顧起來，與我們通常想象的事物的自然程序相反，它的創作是攝影在先，故事在后。

　　按照思路，有一位僧帶着三個疑惑，和一位女神帶着三個渴望她想轉化成一個人，我請來我兩位素未謀過面的朋友拍攝。規則是在拍攝過程中，他們不能交談。除了極少的機會以外也不能互視，因爲他們採取的位置是一位要在另一位的前方。他們只能依靠身體接觸，由他們自己來表現動作和對應動作。

　　我們談了一會兒，他們就着妝開始拍攝了，六小時后拍攝完畢。我們没有説話，我們被變化了。對我們三個人來説，這是一次經歷信任、同情、熱愛的轉化和對愛心治愈能力的體驗。我不知道我的那些照片曾揭示什麽，但我懂得通過鏡頭所看見的一切。

　　當我們坐下來看這些照片時，效果是相當令人驚奇的。一張張肖像在低語、吟唱、呼喊，甚至舞蹈，演繹着一個故事讓我得寫出來。隨後幾個月中，我仍然閱覽回味着照片，就象修補匠的鈴兒舞過水面。我把照片收集起來，給出詳細地描述，於是開始了一個啓迪的歷程。我走的歷程和《僧與神》所走的歷程一樣長。

　　我把創作過程所得的禮物與大家一起分享。

for the gift of moonrise

明月升空的禮贊

Imagine the challenge
 of touching another person
with no gaining idea —
 just presence and caring.

— Jon Kabat-Zinn
 <u>Wherever You Go, There You Are</u>

想象一下
在不知不覺中只用出現和關切就感動了別人，
所具有的激勵作用吧。

——喬卡巴特－晉
<u>無論你去哪裏，你就在哪裏。</u>

The Monk and the Goddess

僧與神

Part 1
Doubts

第一部　疑惑

<u>And so it began</u> that there was a monk with three doubts, each rising in intensity.

起初，有一位僧，他有三個翻騰強烈的疑惑。

It was a time of pain that he sat with — alone in stillness. For it was there in stillness, that his heart spoke. In silence, he emptied his mind of clutter. In stillness, he listened to his heart. "Seek out the other," it said. "Seek out the other."

他獨自在寂靜中打坐的時候，是痛苦的。他的心在靜默中訴說。他默默地理平了思緒，靜靜地傾聽着自己的心聲。"找到另一位"，心在說。"找到另一位"。

<u>And so it began</u> that he journeyed for cycles of time on a path of not-knowing. Finally, he arrived at the foot of a mountain. Again, he sat. Doubting. Doubting the existence of the "other" with whom he could be. His silent cry heard only by one, who came. Hers, a quiet gentle presence, that moved both toward sharing what was true. He knew her to be a Bodhisattva. He knew her to be the Goddess of Compassion, a selfless companion to pain. He knew her to be the "other." <u>And so it began</u> for the Monk and the Goddess.

於是，他開始在一個未經之徑作漫長地游歷。最終，他抵達一座高山腳下，重又打坐并疑惑起來，疑惑那"另一位"的存在。他靜靜地哭泣僅被一位女神聽見了。她溫文爾雅地出現，與他分享真理的意義。他知道她是一位善助人間的神明，是憐憫女神，是能分擔痛苦的無私同伴。他明白，她就是那"另一位"。於是，僧和神的故事有了開端。

They sat together, quite still.

他們在一起靜靜地打坐。

She waited. For it would be the Monk who would determine the journey. It would be the monk who would open three gates — allowing in what waited outside. Days passed, moment by moment.

她期待着，要由僧來決定歷程，由僧開啓那三扇大門，使外面的期待進來。時光在分分秒秒地流逝着。

*A Bodhisattva sat present to pain. In time, a Monk gave it over to her. At that moment, a gate opened and **trust** joined them at the foot of the mountain. <u>And so it began</u>.*

在痛苦的時刻，一位神明出現了，僧及時把痛苦移交給她。此時，第一扇大門打開了。在高山腳下，他們彼此建立了信任。

Her compassion touched him with enormous gentleness.

她的同情憐憫之心，以極大的溫柔感動了他。

The Monk responded by wrapping the pain of his second doubt in surrender. The Goddess accepted his pain as a gift, taking it from him and into herself, willingly. With her, he felt worthy. With her, he felt whole. With her, he opened his heart and loved himself. Then, in the glow of evening moonrise, the second gate opened — and mutual entered.

作爲回應，僧不再隱忍并交出他第二個疑惑的痛苦。女神把他的痛苦像禮物一樣悅納，情願地承接給自己。有了她，他感受到價值和完整。有了她，他誠意地愛戀自己。於是，在一個月光皎潔的夜晚，第二扇大門打開，友情進來了。

Many weeks passed, and the final gate remained closed, as the Monk sat with resistance. For his third doubt lived in a place the Monk dreaded — a cave — where the Dragon waited. This doubt, the most ferocious of the three, embodied fear. Fear of intention, of results, of death.

許多星期過去了，最後的大門仍然緊閉，僧固守着。那第三個疑惑是去僧恐懼的地方——一個洞穴，在那裏有龍守護着。這個疑惑，是三個之中最冷酷的，蘊涵着恐懼。憂慮目的，結果，和毀滅。

*The Goddess held him, as a mother with a wounded child, and poured love into his fear —
generous, unselfish love.*

女神攬着他，像母親攬着一個受傷的孩子，將慷慨無私地愛傾注在他的恐懼裏。

Lingering on the edge of awareness, as slight as the sliver of a new moon, a realization began rising in the Monk. She, whom he had come to love as perfection, was he. No longer a delineation of where one ended and the other began. He was the Goddess and she the Monk. Her strength was his strength. Her wisdom, his. One in the same. Then, as with a gust of clear mountain air — the third gate opened and the universe entered.

徘徊在意識的邊緣，僧的裏面升起如新月牙兒一樣清晰地認識，他所愛的完美的她，是他自己。不必描繪在何處一個結束而另一個誕生。他是女神而她是僧。她的力量就是他的力量，她的智慧成爲他的智慧。反之也同樣。於是伴着一陣輕爽的山風——第三扇大門打開了，世界得以進入。

Thus, armed with the wisdom of a Bodhisattva and the strength of a warrior, the Monk ventured forth to the cave of the Dragon. He entered not to engage in mortal combat, but rather to sit in the presence of his fear, in a way that was welcoming. No confrontation, no deeds of trickery. No fire bolts or hissing. Simply present. Each to the other. Moment by moment.

在神明的智慧和勇士的力量武裝下，僧前去龍守護的洞穴探險。他進去沒有進行格鬥，而是以一種欣然的方式面對他的恐懼坐下來。沒有對抗，沒有騙術。沒有激發閃電或噓唏聲。只是單純地相互呈現。時間就這樣過去了。

Upon his return, he rested in the arms of the Goddess, grateful for all she had offered him. He slept soundly. When he awoke, he found her gone — and yet not. <u>And so it began</u>, the Monk's journey with the "other" — a companion of self.

他回來了,歇息在女神的臂彎中,感激她所給予的一切。他酣睡過去。當他醒來時,發現她還沒有走。於是僧與"另一位"——自己的伴侶開始了一個共同的歷程。

Part II
Longings

第二部　渴望

In the cycles of time that followed, the Goddess continued her journey of open-hearted compassion. Yet within her, there seemed a question that was more than a matter of curiosity. A question of experiencing the human condition. If she chose to transform herself into a human, hers would be a decision of intention — to experience the raw and tender energy of the human spirit. To experience the loving kindness and compassion of another. She would not be guided by her Bodhisattva wisdom, but would leave it behind and begin a new journey of awakening. <u>And thus</u>, <u>it came to pass</u> that a Goddess became a woman. A woman alone, wandering with her longings. Three longings. Each rising in intensity.

在隨後的日子裏，女神繼續走她全心全意憐憫的歷程。而在她裏面除了好奇似乎還有一個問題。一個體驗人世的問題。如果她選擇把自己轉化成一個人，她就要有意識地決定去經歷人類靈魂那原始脆弱的能力。去體驗別人的關愛和同情。她將不必用神明的智慧作引導，將其放在次要的位置上而開始一個全新的覺醒的歷程。如此，女神變成了一個女人。一個孤獨的女人，帶着她的三個強烈地渴望漫游。

On the fourth day of the new moon, she came upon a Monk. She was drawn to him like evening mist to the mountaintop. With him, she felt a connection to life and its goodness — an ease of presence that encouraged the blossoming of trust.

在新月兒的第四天,她突遇一位僧。她像夜晚的薄霧繞在山頂上一樣被他所吸引。與他在一起,她感受到一種與生命的聯結以及安然存在能促進信任的真諦。

<u>And thus, it came to pass</u> that a woman and a Monk began a spiritual journey of enlightenment — together — like sunshine and moonrise. A cycle of complement, teaching and learning one to the other. A lesson of loving kindness and compassion that seemed somehow familiar to both. Her first longing, gone.

　　於是，一個女人和一位僧開始了一個心靈交融的歷程，明朗得如同陽光照耀和明月當空。他們不斷地相互贊賞，教導和學習對方，他們似乎都懂得慈愛和同情。她的第一個渴望滿足了。

In the months that followed, every breath, every moment held a sense of exhilaration filled with the joy of awakening. All things bright, new, thrilling. There existed a natural harmony between these two. Gifts freely given, and received with gratitude.

　　幾個月過去，每時每刻都充滿了歡樂和覺醒的喜悅。所有的事情都是燦爛的，新穎的，令人振奮的。在他們兩人之間存在一種天然地和諧。慷慨地贈送禮物，和心懷感激地接受。

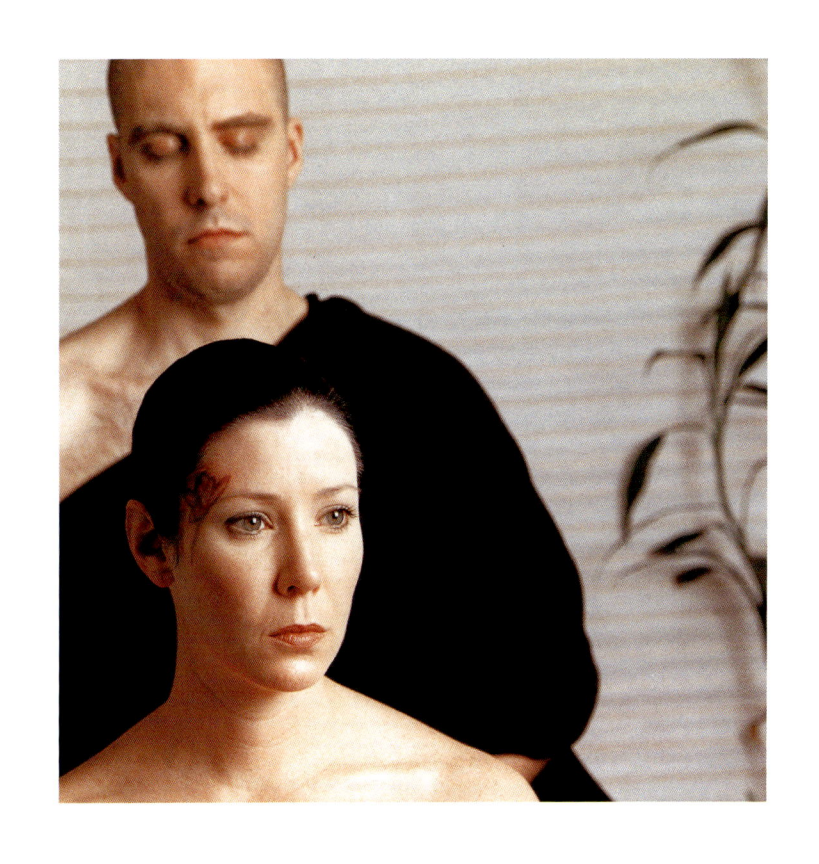

Then, light and shadow, opposites occupying the same space, wedged between the woman and the Monk. Like a jealous child, her second longing demanded attention. A longing for permanence. A desire for something lasting.

爾後，光亮和暗影這兩個對立的事物占據了同一個空間，嵌在女人和僧之間。像一個忌妒的孩子一樣，她的第二個渴望需要被關注。這是對持久的渴望，期望事物的永恆。

Suddenly, a teacher with a difficult lesson to be taught. A student, with difficult words yet to be heard.

一個老師突然遇到一個難講的課題，一個學生聽到難懂的字眼。

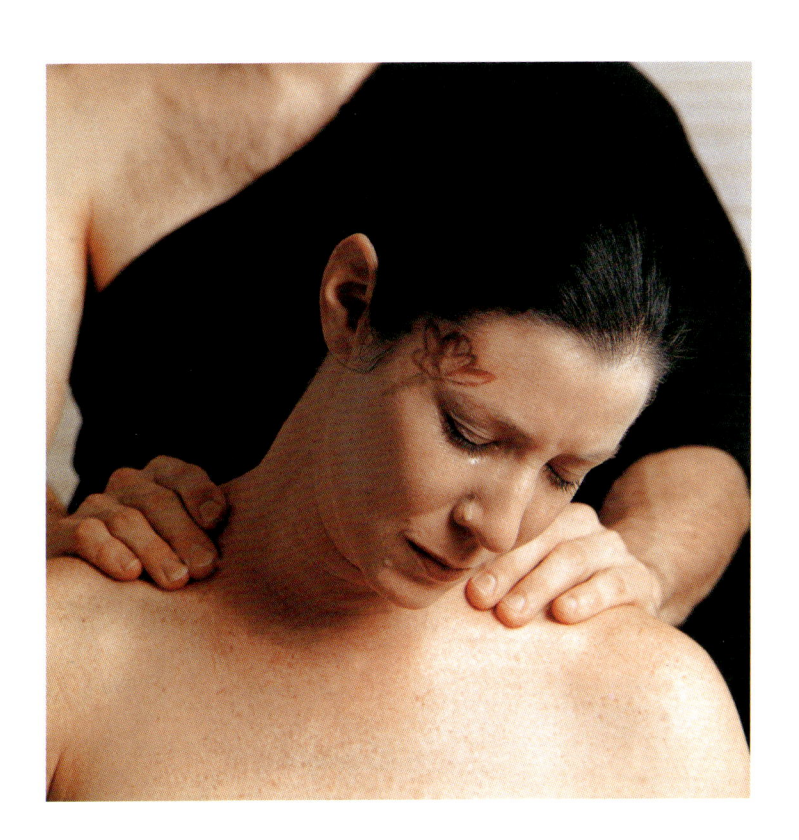

Light and shadow beckoned, leading her into a darkness the woman dreaded.

光亮和暗影引導着她走進一個女人恐懼的黑暗之中。

And thus, it came to pass that a Monk sat present to pain. A woman gave it over to him.

在女人痛苦的時候，僧出現了。女人把痛苦交給他。

僧

The Monk offered her his candle. She took it, and with her first step, he blew it out. And so, she began her journey to where things fall apart. A groundless, hopeless lonely place.

僧給了她蠟燭。 她拿着蠟燭邁出第一步，他吹熄了蠟燭。於是，她開始她的旅程，去那事物離散的地方，一個無根無望寂寞的地方。

The days were long in her absence.

没有她的日子是漫長的。

For the Monk, her return was a love affair with newness, like the fresh scent of rain in the forest or the way snow holds light on the mountains. She spoke with gentleness about how the path to understanding had been dark and frightening.

對於僧來說，她的歸來是一種新生的愛情，像森林中雨水的清新氣味；像高山上的白雪映亮的路。她温柔地講述着通往理解的小路是如何的黑暗和恐怖。

神

She had returned to the Monk with a gift and bowed as she presented it to him. Carefully, he opened it. The box appeared empty, yet he felt its fullness. Nestled within the emptiness was her gift of the moment — <u>this moment</u> — wrapped in her awareness that nothing lasts — making this gift more loving, more intimate, more filled with gratitude than either of them had ever shared.

　　她給僧帶回一個禮物，她躬身遞給僧。僧仔細地打開禮物。盒子似乎是空的，但他覺得是充滿着的。她的這一時刻就是駐在這盒子中的禮物。這一時刻，覆蓋在她的意識裏：世界上沒有永恒的存在——使這件禮物比他們以往分享的任何一件禮物更可愛，更精美，更充滿感激。

"No matter what the relationship," she said softly, *"we depart from each other. The sum total of what we have — ever — is our presence to the moment."*
"Yes," he nodded. *"I know."*

"無論關係是什么"，她輕輕地說，"我們要彼此分開。總之，我們曾經所擁有的是——我們在那一時刻出現"。"是的"，他點着頭。"我知道"。

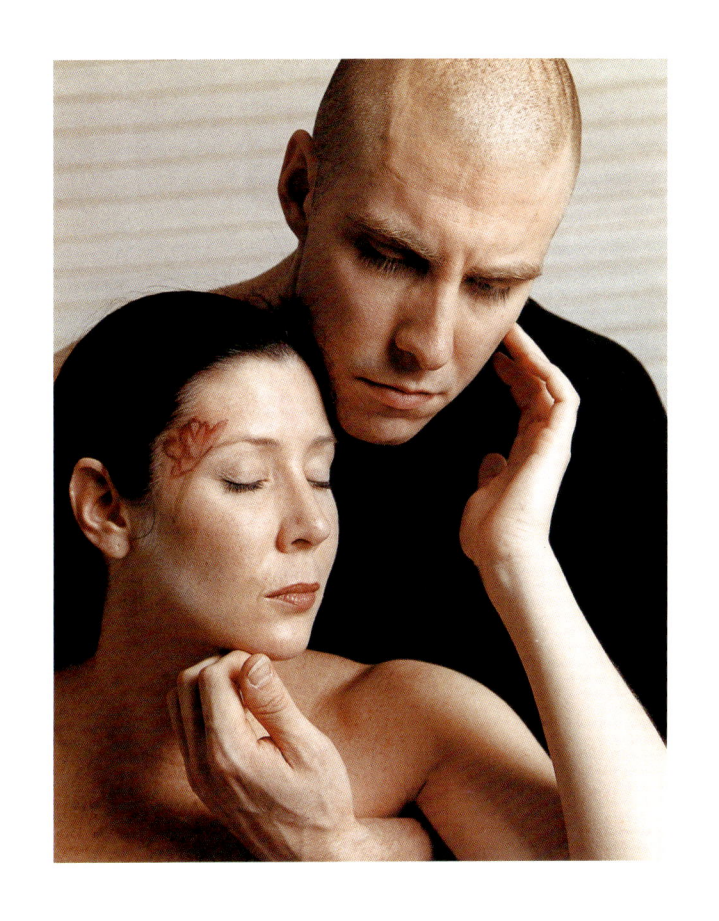

She reached up and touched his face, and he hers. A duet in perfect harmony — one they had sung before.

　　她向上撫摸他的臉，他也撫摸她的臉。這是一支他們以前唱過的優美和諧的二步曲。

Her third longing arrived as a messenger of time, requesting a decision — one that required remembrance. Would she return to her existence as a Goddess, or was there more to be learned by staying? Stay or go — opposites sharing the same space equally.

她的第三個渴望像時光的信使一樣來到了。要求作一個要記憶的決定。她是回到她作女神的生活裏，還是學着留下來過活？留或去——兩個相反的實際平分了同一個空間。

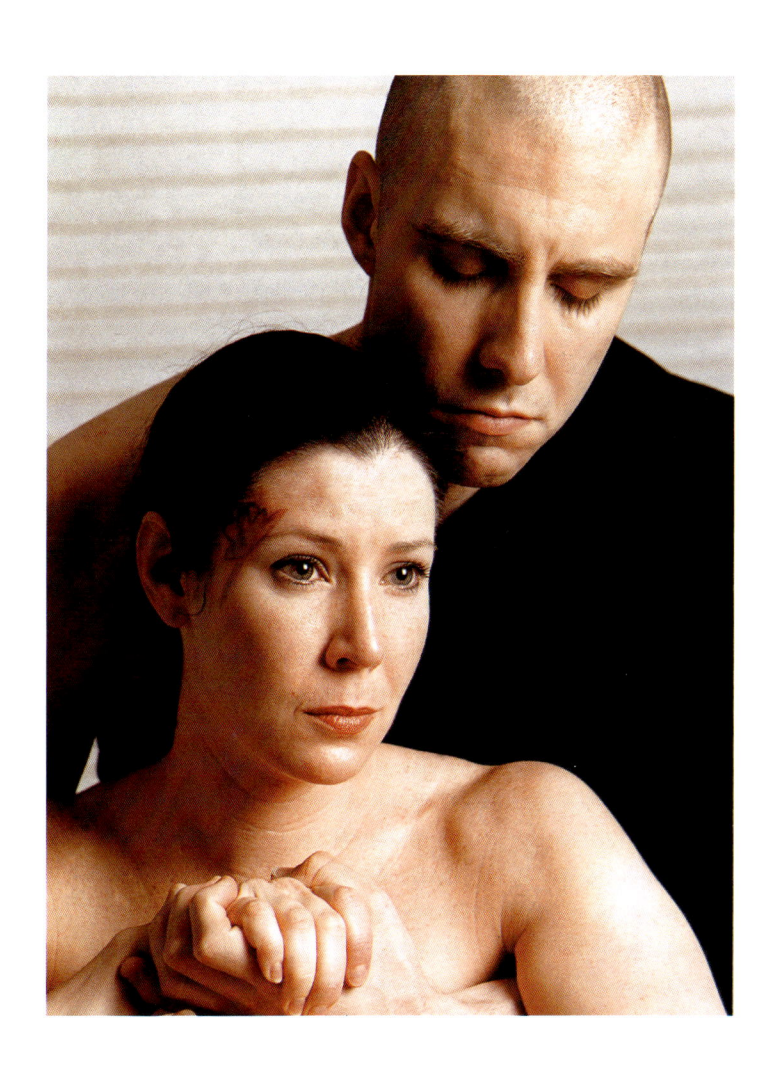

Remembering now how it all began, with a Monk and his doubts, she longed for both — staying and going.

回想起這一切的開端,與帶着疑惑的僧,她渴望留,也渴望去。

The hours wove themselves into days and the days into weeks, as she and the Monk talked of the messenger's arrival, of a time shared at the foot of a mountain, of decisions to be made. They sat together in stillness. For it was in stillness that their hearts spoke. Her longing remained before them, like a sentinel guarding what lay beyond.

當她和僧談着信使的到來，在高山脚下分享的時光，和需要作出的決定時，日子已經一天天，一周周慢慢地過去了。他們静静地坐在一起，在寂静中，他們的心在交流。她的渴望仍然像一位哨兵守護在他們的前方。

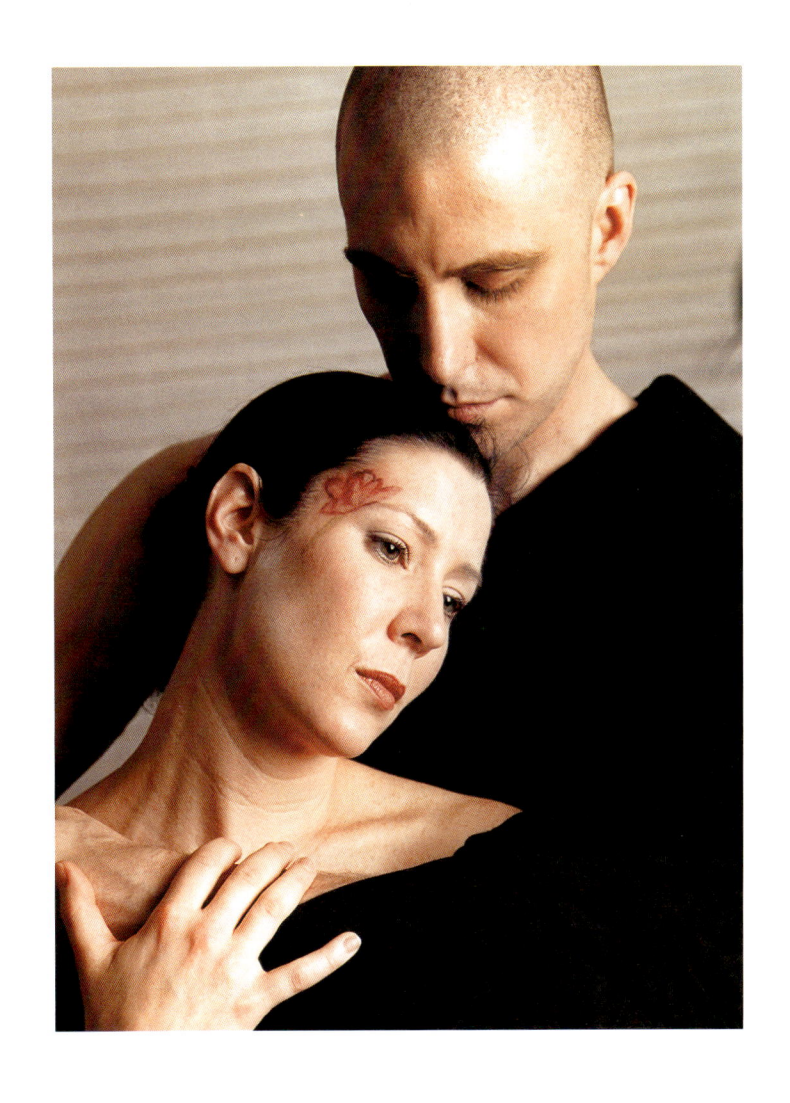

They stood, facing the moment like leaves of grass woven together with no anticipation of wind or storm. A decision made. A messenger sent back with a reply to time.

他們站起來，面對這樣的時刻就像草葉兒在無暴風雨的時候盤旋在一起。決定作出來了。信使把這個決定帶回給時光。

They stood present to their feelings — both human and honest. They stood present to each other, mutual. So simple, and yet — so difficult.

他們站立着，面對他們自己的感覺——人性和誠信。他們相對而立。如此簡單，而又如此不易。

<u>And thus, it came to pass</u>, that there lived a man who was a monk and a woman who was a goddess.

　　於是，那裏開始生活着一個男人他曾是一位僧，和一個女人她曾是一位女神。

Author Photograph by Gary Collings

Anne Knoll, photographer, writer, performer, director combines these talents in her creative work. The concept of "mute eloquence" continues to be the driving force for her photography. She believes that there is in each of us passion, poetry, music, and a longing to share — if only for a moment — what lies beneath. As a photographer, she approaches those moments with a sense of honesty and integrity — simply and with gratitude.

Ms. Knoll is the author of several children's stories including two in a series on adoption, and a book of poetry. All were printed as limited editions and sold in bookstores and galleries. She lives and works in New Jersey.

Website: www.MonkAndGoddess.com
Email: anne@knollphotos.com
Phone toll free: 1-866-354-8512

安－諾奧，是攝影家、作家、表演藝術家、導演，集所有這些才能于她的作品中。"緘默而富雄辯力"的概念仍然是她搞攝影的驅動力量。她相信我們每個人都有可分享的激情、詩歌、音樂，以及對某一時刻意味的渴望。作爲一位攝影家，她用一種誠實正直的感覺，單純而又充滿感謝地探討這些時刻。

安－諾奧寫過幾部兒童小說，其中兩部爲長篇小說，和一部詩集。這些作品限數出版，在書店和書畫陳列室面市。她在美國新澤西州生活和工作。

Special thanks to each of the following — and so many more — for their open-hearted generosity and support!

Friends

Mary Carle
Marie Carpentier
Chuck Crawley
Bruce & Kimberly Curless
Ingrid Damiani
Brenda & Chuck Driben
Karen & Bruce Dyer
Express It Copying Center
The Fabulous Five
Feihong Song / New China Book Store
Esther Flaster
Bob & Wendy Grady
Mimi Gallicchio
Mary Graham
David Greene
Gulla Auto Tag Service, Inc.
Fred & Joanne Hickman
Lyn & John Knepler
Jeremy Knoll & Jennifer Denn
Melissa Knoll & Ted Dezvane
Martha Lavey
Mary Ellen Nudd
Anne Marie Offer
Patt Osborne & Bob Rader
Ken & Mary Lou Previti
Renee Previti
Robert Michael Communications
Ann Smith
Mary St. Martin

The Solstice Sisters
Lois Staas
Mark Taylor
The Thai Garden Restaurant
Bendt & Ellen Themstrup
Al & Ginny Waters
Laurel Eckhardt Wilson

Benefactors

Howard & Caroline Alber
Herman Knoll
Rosalyn Miller
Mike & Jeanine Zaikowski

朋友

林惠冰、張文琴
丁妮（文迪框畫公司）
劉雪梅
林國斌
江氏藝術服務公司
華光文藝中心

瓊華酒樓

For inquiries and order requests
please contact
Website: www.MonkAndGoddess.com
Email: anne@knollphotos.com
Phone toll free: 1-866-354-8512